En parejas   *2*

A Four-Book Series of Communicative Activities

Lucía Caycedo Garner

University of Wisconsin—Madison

Debbie Rusch

Boston College

Marcela Domínguez

University of California, Los Angeles

Houghton Mifflin Company   Boston

Dallas   Geneva, Illinois   Palo Alto   Princeton, New Jersey

Illustrations by Walt Fournier
Activities 4, 6, 7, 9, 10, 12, 15, 17, 18, 21, 23

Illustrations by Stephanie O'Shaughnessy
Activities 2, 3, 8, 11, 14, 19, 24

Photographs
Activity 8: AP/Wide World Photos
Activity 22: (boy) Jeffrey Myers, Stock Boston
(girl) Spencer Grant, Stock Boston

Cover design by Darci Mehall

Printed in the U.S.A.

ISBN: 0–395–55429–2

Library of Congress Catalog Card Number: 90–83013

CDEFGHIJ-B-99876

Contents

Actividad 6: Objeto olvidado

Communicative functions	Language focus	Topics and vocabulary
Describing objects . Indicating location . Saying when and how something was lost	Preterit . Imperfect . Adjective agreement	Time expressions . Descriptive adjectives

Actividad 7: Objetos perdidos

Communicative functions	Language focus	Topics and vocabulary
Describing objects . Saying where, when, and how something was lost	Preterit . Imperfect . Adjective agreement	Time expressions . Descriptive adjectives

Actividad 8: ¿Quién era?

Communicative functions	Language focus	Topics and vocabulary
Giving personal information . Describing appearance and activities	Preterit . Imperfect . Adjective agreement	Time expressions . Physical characteristics . Occupations . Nationalities

Actividad 9: Mirando fotos

Communicative functions	Language focus	Topics and vocabulary
Describing the weather and vacation activities	Preterit . Imperfect . Question formation	**Hacía** + *weather expressions* . **¿Qué tiempo hacía?** . Leisure-time activities

Actividad 10: Gordos Anónimos

Communicative functions	Language focus	Topics and vocabulary
Comparing the past with the present	Preterit . Imperfect . Simple present . Adjective agreement	Parts of the body . Clothing . Descriptive adjectives . Habitual activities

Actividad 11: La gente curiosa quiere saber

Communicative functions	Language focus	Topics and vocabulary
Asking questions . Giving answers . Discussing one's past and stating future plans	Preterit . Imperfect	Family relationships . **Ir a** + *infinitive*

To the Instructor

En parejas is a four-book series of communicative activities designed to supplement the first two years of a college or university Spanish program or all four years of a high-school program. The underlying premise of the series is that students learn best by doing. *En parejas* offers elementary and intermediate students of Spanish interesting communicative activities that provide realistic practice of important language functions. The information gap format, in which pairs of students perform tasks simultaneously on the basis of differing information, increases student communication time and provides a natural motivation for speaking. These activities provide an important support for achieving effective student-to-student interaction.

Description of the Series

Each book is divided into two sections: the first part for student A and the second part, which is upside down, for student B. Each student has a different set of information needed to carry out a task; for example, when making reservations, student A has a train schedule and student B has a description of the destination and times he/she must inquire about. The instructions for each student are separated in order to create the information gap.

The activities in each book practice the high-frequency functions, grammar points, and vocabulary covered in most texts. The use of pair activities decreases student anxiety and increases speaking time, thereby providing an environment that is conducive to language learning. This is in keeping with the goals of the oral proficiency movement and current trends in language teaching.

How to Use En parejas

Student Responsibilities

In order to receive the maximum benefit from the use of pair activities, encourage students to have fun and to use their imagination. They should know that they are active participants in their own learning process and that, during pairwork, they have the following responsibilities:

1. to work cooperatively.

2. to look only at their own information and not to peek at their partner's book.

3. to enunciate and speak clearly and to insist on clear pronunciation from their partner.

4. to ask for clarification if needed.

5. to correct each other's grammar when necessary.

6.   to use their hands to gesture unless specifically instructed otherwise.

Once students recognize their responsibilities during pair work, anxiety will decrease and a productive environment will be established.

Selecting an Activity

En parejas is intended to enhance classroom teaching. The activities are designed to be used either as culminating activities after studying a particular function, grammar point or word set, or as reentry of already learned items. Students should already have worked with and should be familiar with the structures and vocabulary needed to carry out the task. The activities are not meant to be used during the introductory or drill phase of instruction. If students are well-prepared before doing an activity, errors should be minimal and should not impede communication.

Although the order of activities is in keeping with the sequences commonly presented in many textbooks, the activities may be done in any order as dictated by the course syllabus and the judgment of the instructor. The table of contents indicates which functions, grammar points, and vocabulary are needed to carry out each activity. Consult the table of contents to choose activities that are appropriate for the topic being covered in the classroom. High-frequency functions are practiced more than once, allowing the students to apply their knowledge to a variety of situations.

Forming Pairs

Vary partners frequently so that students are constantly working with different members of the class. Here are a few suggestions for forming pairs:

1.   Pair students according to ability: stronger students with weaker ones or strong with strong.

2.   Pair students randomly:

    a. Divide the class in half and have students number off; then number 1 works with number 1, number 2 with number 2, etc.

    b. Students choose their partner themselves.

    c. Arrange students alphabetically: pair students from opposite ends of the alphabet or according to the class roster.

3.   Arrange groups by sex: males with males or males with females.

For classes with an odd number of students, have one group of three students work together with two of the students doubling up to work one part; have one student monitor a pair of students; or, place three students who work quickly in one group, thus allowing them to do the activity twice.

It is not recommended that you pair yourself with the extra student, since you should monitor all groups, answer any questions that come up, and make sure that all students are on task and actively engaged.

Many of the activities in the series simulate real-life situations. In order to help students visualize the scene, have them recreate the situation as much as possible. For example, when simulating a phone conversation, students can sit back to back. Or, if recreating a scene in a store, one student can stand behind his/her desk, which represents a counter.

Introducing an Activity

Before beginning an activity, make sure students understand the function or functions being practiced and the grammar and vocabulary needed to carry out the functions. Pay special attention to the useful expressions that are given at the beginning of each activity.

To ensure that each student knows exactly what his/her role is, read through the directions with the students or have the students read through the directions alone. Circulate at the beginning of the activity to make sure all students are working appropriately on the task. It is also possible to model the beginning of an activity with a student or to have two students model the activity before having the whole class begin.

In order to ensure that all students become involved immediately, set a time limit on the activity. Students will attack the task with more vigor if the time limit is a little bit less than what actually may be needed. For example, if an activity should take approximately seven minutes, set a time limit of five minutes. Since some activities are open-ended, it is important for students to know how much time they have.

If a follow-up activity is going to be done (such as reporting back to the class with your findings, writing a newspaper article about the person you are interviewing, etc.), make sure this is clear before beginning.

While an Activity Is in Progress

It is important to monitor pair activities. At this time you may do any or all of the following things:

1. Make sure students are on task.

2. Offer suggestions.

3. Answer questions.

4. Correct individual errors when communication is impeded.

5. Note grammatical errors for further classroom work.

6. Note problem areas of pronunciation for further classroom work.

While an activity is in progress, you must decide when to stop the activity. It is not necessary that all groups finish each activity. Just playing the game can be more important than winning. When two or three groups have finished, they can either reverse roles or you can end the activity for the whole class.

Wrapping Up an Activity

No matter how you choose to end an activity, it is important that the students know how they will be held accountable for what is accomplished during the pair activity. Here are a few suggestions for wrap-up activities:

1. Have individuals report their findings to the class. The first activity in each book allows students to get to know each other. A group sharing at this point may be quite productive to reduce anxiety.

2. Identify a group that has done something humorous and have them share with their peers, either by reporting back or by acting out the activity for the class.

3. Many activities can be self-checked by having pairs compare their completed activity (pictures, lists, data, etc.).

4. Collect and correct for accuracy activities that require a specific interchange of data.

5. Assign a brief composition, newspaper article, follow-up letter, etc., based on the contents of the activity.

Advantages of Pairwork

Frequent use of interactive pairwork activities provides a variety of benefits, including the following:

1. Students learn to depend on and learn from each other through cooperative interaction.

2. Self-esteem is fostered: every student is important and vital to the interaction.

3. Student motivation increases since every student must participate in the activity.

4. Class dynamics improve.

5. As students gain confidence in their abilities, their fear of speaking decreases and motivation increases.

6. Individual creativity and imagination are encouraged.

7. Problem-solving skills are strengthened.

8. The foreign language becomes a natural means to convey real meaning and personal ideas.

9. Students learn to have fun and express humor in Spanish.

10. The language learning process becomes enjoyable and self-directed.

En parejas   2

ESTUDIANTE A

Actividad 1: ¿Y tú quién eres?

Fill out the following form with information about yourself.

Nombre: _____	Apellido: _____
Dirección: _____
Ciudad: _____	Teléfono: _____
Casa: _____ Apartamento: _____	Otro: _____
Origen de tu familia: _____
Comida favorita: _____	Actor/actriz favorito/a: _____
Deportes que practicas: _____
Película favorita: _____
Pasatiempo favorito: _____
Asignatura favorita: _____	Asignatura que menos te gusta: _____

You begin by asking your partner questions to complete the following card. When you finish, your partner will ask you questions. Ask questions such as:

¿Cómo te llamas?
¿Cuál es tu dirección?
¿Cuál es tu comida favorita?

Nombre: _____	Apellido: _____
Dirección: _____
Ciudad: _____	Teléfono: _____
Casa: _____ Apartamento: _____	Otro: _____
Origen de tu familia: _____
Comida favorita: _____	Actor/actriz favorito/a: _____
Deportes que practicas: _____
Película favorita: _____
Pasatiempo favorito: _____
Asignatura favorita: _____	Asignatura que menos te gusta: _____

Actividad 2: La cita con el médico

You are calling on the telephone to make an appointment with Doctor Malahierba.
Use expressions such as:

Quisiera hacer una cita . . .
A las 10:00 es imposible porque . . .
No puedo a esa hora porque tengo que . . .
¿Puedo ir el lunes a las . . . ?

Your partner will begin. The following is your schedule for the week:

MARZO

lunes 1/3 9:00 -10:30 Clase de historia
            1:00 Almuerzo con Carlos

martes 2/3 10:00 - 11:00 Tenis en el club
             12:00 - 3:00 Estudiar para examen

miércoles 3/3 8:30 - 10:15 Examen de historia
                Llamar a Carolina entre las 2:00 y las 4:00
                4:00 - 6:00 Ver el concierto de Sting por TV

jueves 4/3 9:00 - 10:00 Tenis en el club

viernes 5/3 Fiesta de Patricia 8:00 p.m.

Actividad 3:   La cita con el dentista

You are Doctora Dientesano's secretary. A patient calls to make an appointment to see the dentist. Helpful expressions include:

> **La doctora no trabaja por las mañanas.**
> **La primera hora libre es a las . . .**
> **La última hora libre es . . .**
> **Ya tiene otra cita a las . . .**
> **Tiene libre el . . . a las . . .**
> **¿Qué tal el . . . a las . . . ?**

Begin the conversation by saying: *Consultorio, buenos días.*

Here is her appointment book:

junio

lunes 16/6		martes 17/6	
16:00	Sr. Pérez	16:00	Sra. Martínez
16:30	Pilar Rodríguez	16:30	Pepe Delgado
17:00		17:00	Julio Delgado
17:30	Juan Lerma	17:30	Juan Lerma
18:00		18:00	
18:30		18:30	

miércoles 18/6		jueves 19/6	
16:00		16:00	Ramón Cano
16:30	Isabel Sánchez	16:30	Pilar Rodríguez
17:00		17:00	
17:30		17:30	Juan Lerma
18:00	Juan Lerma	18:00	
18:30		18:30	

Boca limpia, sonrisa feliz

Actividad 4: El coche perfecto

You and your friend have just purchased new cars. Your partner is always bragging about his/her things, but this time you know that your car is better than his/hers. Compare specific features about the two cars. Use expressions such as:

¿Cuántos cilindros . . . ?   El mío tiene más . . .
¿Tiene . . . ?   El tuyo tiene menos . . .
El mío es mejor porque . . .   Me gusta más . . .
El tuyo es peor porque . . .   El mío es tan . . . como el tuyo.

Your partner will begin.

Fantasma un coche para el año 2000

- Usa 6 litros de gasolina cada 100 kilómetros
- Va de 0 a 100 kilómetros en 6,5 segundos
- Descapotable
- 2 puertas
- Radiocassette estéreo
- Aire acondicionado

- Llantas Michelín
- Motor de 6 cilindros
- De 5 marchas
- Asientos de cuero
- Espejo retrovisor al lado del pasajero
- Limpiaparabrisas con 3 velocidades (rápida, normal, intermitente)
- Color del coche: rojo

Actividad 5: La tarea

You need to find out some information for your class *Geografía del hemisferio occidental*. In order to complete your assignment quickly, you split the work with your partner. Find out what your partner has learned from his/her research and complete the chart below. Use phrases such as: **¿Sabes cuántos . . . ?   ¿Me puedes decir cuántos . . . ?**

Your partner will begin.

Geografía del hemisferio occidental

Países:	Número de habitantes
Brasil	_____
Estados Unidos	247.100.000
México	_____
Ciudades:	
Nueva York	14.598.000
San Pablo	_____
México	16.901.000
Territorio:	**Kilómetros cuadrados**
Brasil	_____
Canadá	9.970.610
Estados Unidos sin Alaska y Hawai	_____
Ríos:	**Kilómetros de largo**
Paraná	3.999
Amazonas	_____
Misisipí	3.779
Volcanes activos:	**Metros de altura**
Guallatiri, Chile	_____
Lascar, Chile	5.994
Cotopaxi, Ecuador	_____
Cataratas:	**Metros de altura**
Salto Ángel, Venezuela	807
Cuquenán, Venezuela	_____
King George, Guayana	488

Brasil

Estados Unidos

Now that you have completed the data, quiz each other by trying to formulate and answer some of the questions that might be on the test. Questions may include: **¿Cuál es el río más . . . ?   ¿Cuál es más alto/a, . . . ?   ¿Cuál es más grande, . . . o . . . ?   ¿Cuál tiene mayor población, . . . o . . . ?**

You will begin.

Actividad 6: Objeto olvidado

You have forgotten your gym bag in the locker room of your gym and you go back to claim it. Explain how and where you left it and describe the contents of your bag. Use expressions such as:

> Olvidé el . . .
> El bolso era . . .
> Tenía unas medias . . .

You begin by saying:

> *Perdón, olvidé un bolso en el vestuario y quisiera saber si Ud. lo tiene.*

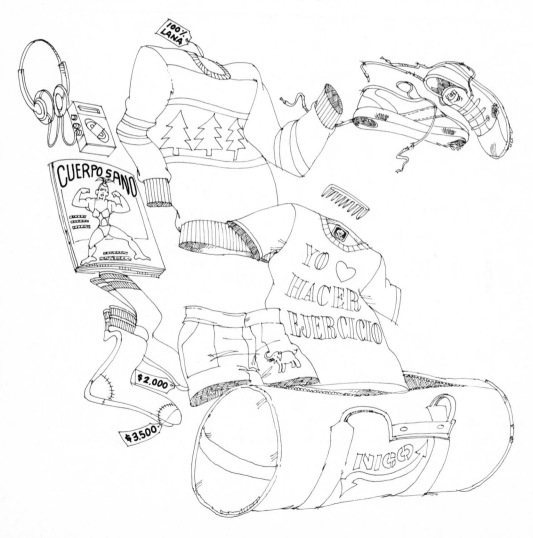

Actividad 7:   Objetos perdidos

You are a clerk in the lost-and-found office at a bus station. A passenger comes to your office to report lost luggage. Ask questions to fill out a report. Make sure you get a detailed description of what was lost. Use expressions such as:

¿Dónde estaba?
¿Qué tenía en . . . ?
¿Cuántas . . . había?
¿De qué color era . . . ?

Your partner will begin.

Estación de Autobuses Retiro
Avda. 11 de Julio 2346
Santiago de Chile

Fecha: _____

Nombre: _____

Dirección: _____

Ciudad: _____

Teléfono: _____

Objeto(s) perdido(s): _____

Descripción (color, tamaño, cantidad): _____

_____

_____

_____

Dónde: _____

Cuándo: _____

Comentarios: _____

_____

Actividad 8: ¿Quién era?

Think of a famous person who is no longer living and whom you think your partner would know. Your partner will ask you questions to determine which famous person you have in mind. For the first ten questions you may answer only **sí** or **no**, but after that, your partner may ask you questions to get specific information. When your partner has figured out who the person is, switch roles. Useful expressions include:

¿Vivió en este siglo?
¿Era hombre / mujer?
¿Era abogado / médico / etc.?
¿Tenía pelo rubio / castaño / etc.?

You may want to make a game of this by awarding a point for each question asked. The person who guesses correctly asking the least number of questions is the winner.

Your partner will begin.

Some suggestions follow:

John Kennedy	Lucille Ball
Cleopatra	Charlie Chaplin
Cristóbal Colón	Salvador Dalí

You have just returned from your Christmas vacation with some friends and are discussing your vacation with another friend, who has also just returned from a vacation. You spent five days in southern Spain. Tell what the weather was like and what you did each day. Then say whether or not you enjoyed the trip. Base your description on the photos below. Take a few minutes to create details surrounding your trip: who went with you, what you did in each place, how you liked it, etc. Use expressions such as:

Fuimos a . . .   **Mientras nosotros . . . de repente . . .**
Era muy bonito; había . . .   **Después . . .**
Me gustó porque . . .   **Al día siguiente . . .**
Hacía calor; por eso . . .   **Más tarde . . .**

You begin by asking: *¿Qué tal pasaste las vacaciones?*

Día 1   Sierra Nevada

Día 2

TABLAO
Flamenco

Autocares de Andalucía

28/12/91	8:30
Granada	10:30
Marbella	20:00
Marbella	22:30
Granada	
	Pts. 2.500

Día 3   Playa de Marbella

Día 4 La Alhambra – Palacio moro, Siglo XIII

Catedral de Granada – Tumbas de Isabel y Fernando (los Reyes Católicos)

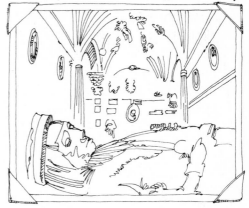

Día 5

PATIO Andaluz
RESTAURANTE CON AMBIENTE TÍPICO
* música ambiental

Actividad 10:   Gordos Anónimos

You are interviewing someone who has lost a lot of weight so that you can write an article for the magazine *Gordos Anónimos*. Find out what the person used to do, what he looked like before losing weight, and what he does now. Use expressions such as:

¿Qué hacía Ud. cuando . . . ?
¿Comía . . . ?
¿Cómo empezó a bajar de peso?
Ahora, ¿qué tipo de ejercicio . . . ?

You begin by saying: *¡Qué delgado está Ud.! ¿Cómo lo hizo?*

Fecha:
Nombre:
Lugar de la entrevista:

Descripción física:
Antes

Ahora

Hábitos:
Antes

Ahora

Anécdota interesante:

Actividad 11: La gente curiosa quiere saber

You are Elvira Milaños. You are going to be interviewed on the talk show "Cuénteselo a millones." You are 95 years old and have just divorced your 97-year-old husband, Pancracio, after seventy-two years of marriage. You are ecstatic about your new-found freedom. The first three years of your marriage were great, but trouble started after that. You had always wanted to divorce your husband, but you stayed together for the children. When your youngest child died last month, you finally decided to go ahead with a divorce. Look at the following drawings to help you discuss your marriage, your divorce, and your plans for the future. Use expressions such as: **Cuando nos casamos yo . . .   Después de los primeros tres años, él empezó a . . .   Me molestaba mucho cuando . . .   Siempre . . .   Nunca . . .   Ahora voy a . . .   Quiero . . .**

Your partner will begin.

Razones para casarte hace 72 años:

Primeros tres años de casada:

Razones para divorciarte:

Planes futuros:

Divorciada, 95 años, delgada, pelo blanco, baila rumba, salsa y lambada. Busca hombre soltero, divorciado o viudo, activo, de 70 a 90 años con coche deportivo rojo. Delgado pero musculoso.

Actividad 12:   Contando la historia

The following pictures tell a story. In order to complete the story and find out every-thing that happened, you will need to talk to your partner, who has the missing pictures. When you finish, give the story a title. Use expressions such as:

El hombre fue a correr . . .
(Él) estaba corriendo y de repente . . .
Mientras él corría . . .

You begin by saying: *Un señor estaba en el cuarto de baño . . .*

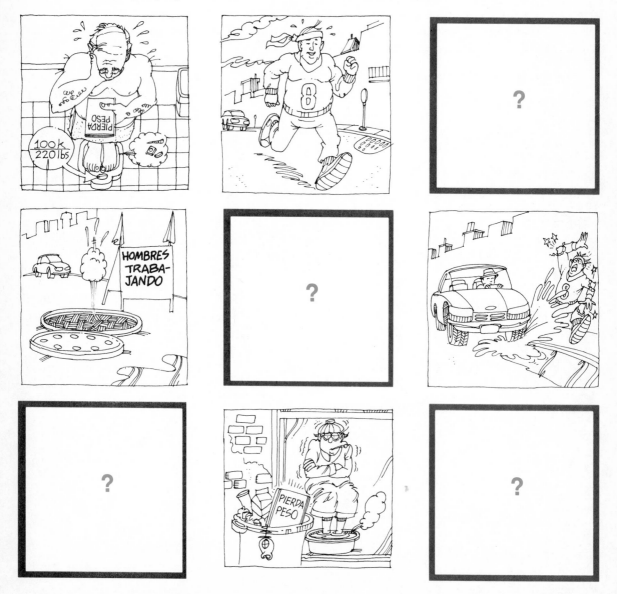

Actividad 13: Una conversación

You have a list of expressions below. Your partner has a different list of expressions. You and your partner are going to have a logical conversation about any topic you want. Each of you must try to use all the expressions on your list. You may use them in any order you like. The first to use all the expressions is the winner.

Your partner will begin and you will answer, using the following lines:

> *Tu compañero/a:* . . .
> *Tú:* **Fue un día muy interesante.**
> *Tu compañero/a:* . . .
> *Tú:* **Primero, me levanté tarde.**
> *Tu compañero/a:* ???

Here are the expressions you must use in your conversation:

> **De repente yo . . .**
> **Anoche nosotros fuimos . . .**
> **Mientras tanto yo . . .**
> **¡No me digas!**
> **Todos los días . . .**
> **Mañana vamos a . . .**
> **¡Imposible!**
> **Era la una y media cuando . . .**
> **Tuve que hacerlo porque . . .**
> **Lo conocí cuando . . .**

Actividad 14: Completa el dibujo

Below you have a grid with drawings in some of the boxes. Your partner has the missing drawings. In order to complete the entire grid with the correct drawing in each box, you will need to ask your partner questions. Alternate asking questions to complete your grids. Drawings should be simple. Use stick figures if you like.

To give information, use phrases such as: **Dibuja un/a . . . entre . . .**
Baja dos cuadrados y dobla a la . . .

To ask questions, use phrases such as: **¿Dónde está . . . ?**
¿Está encima de . . . ?
¿Está a la derecha de . . . ?

Your partner will begin.

Actividad 15: ¿Sabe Ud. dónde está . . . ?

You are at the Hotel Roma in Lima, Peru, and you want to know how to get to the places listed below. You are eating breakfast at the hotel and you ask the person at the next table for directions. You may use expressions such as:

¿Sabe Ud. dónde está . . . ?
¿Puede decirme cómo llegar a . . . ?
Doble a la izquierda . . .

Lugares: *el Museo de la Inquisición, American Express, la Catedral, el Banco de la Nación, el Restaurante Vegetariano.*

You begin by saying: *¿Sabe Ud. dónde está . . . ?*

¡Ojo! Some streets change names when they cross Unión.

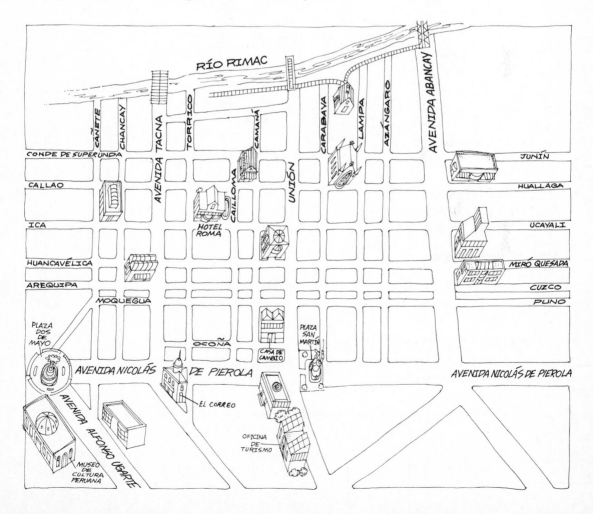

Actividad 16: ¿Te cuidas?

Fill out the following questionnaire about your health and fitness habits. Mark your answers in the box labeled **Tú**.

COMIDA	una vez por semana		tres veces por semana		todos los días	
	Tú	Comp.	Tú	Comp.	Tú	Comp.
verduras	☐	☐	☐	☐	☐	☐
pollo/pescado	☐	☐	☐	☐	☐	☐
fruta	☐	☐	☐	☐	☐	☐

BEBIDAS	una vez por día		tres veces por día		más de tres veces por día	
	Tú	Comp.	Tú	Comp.	Tú	Comp.
agua	☐	☐	☐	☐	☐	☐
té sin cafeína	☐	☐	☐	☐	☐	☐
leche	☐	☐	☐	☐	☐	☐
jugos	☐	☐	☐	☐	☐	☐

EJERCICIO FÍSICO	una vez por semana		tres veces por semana		todos los días	
	Tú	Comp.	Tú	Comp.	Tú	Comp.
deportes en equipo	☐	☐	☐	☐	☐	☐
ejercicio aeróbico	☐	☐	☐	☐	☐	☐
montar en bicicleta	☐	☐	☐	☐	☐	☐

When you have finished, ask your partner questions to see what his/her habits are and mark the responses in the box labeled **Comp**. Use expressions such as: **¿Cuántas veces por semana comes . . . ?**

You begin by asking: *¿Cuántas veces por semana comes verduras?*

Once you are finished, total the results and compare your score with your partner's. Follow the instructions below to arrive at your totals and to interpret your answers.

Puntuación de las respuestas:

Por cada marca en la primera columna recibes 1 punto.

Por cada marca en la segunda columna recibes 2 puntos.

Por cada marca en la tercera columna recibes 3 puntos.

Escribe el total de los puntos de tu parte de la prueba: _____

Escribe el total de los puntos de tu compañero/a: _____

30–25	Eres muy saludable. Debes tener el cuerpo de un león.
24–19	Llevas una vida más o menos saludable, pero debes mirar lo que comes con cuidado y hacer más ejercicio.
18–13	Necesitas cambiar tu ritmo de vida o puedes tener problemas en el futuro.
12–7	Hoy mismo debes hacer cambios en tu rutina diaria.
0–6	¿Seguro que leíste bien las preguntas? Si no quieres acabar en un hospital, es mejor que consultes con un médico para cambiar tu dieta y para que te dé un régimen de ejercicio.

Decide which of you leads a healthier life and give your partner advice to help improve his/her lifestyle. Use expressions such as:

Es mejor que tú . . .
Te aconsejo que . . .
Es necesario que . . .

Actividad 17:   Decorando

You are the assistant for an interior decorator who is redoing a client's living room. He/she is going to call you to explain the design. Here is a floor plan of the room and the furniture you have to place in it. As he/she describes the location of each item, draw it in the floor plan. Use expressions such as: **¿Dónde lo pongo?   ¿Y la mesa?**

You begin by saying: *¿Alo?*

Actividad 18: Buscando apartamento

You are looking for a one-bedroom apartment in Mexico City within walking distance of Chapultepec Park and the Paseo de la Reforma. You have marked the area you are interested in on the map below. You know it will be difficult to find what you want and you may have to make some compromises. You don't have much time, but could see two apartments today. You are looking for an apartment with the following features. Call the real-estate agent to see what he/she has to offer you.

- barato ($150.000–$200.000 pesos mensuales)
- balcón
- sin muebles

- con teléfono
- 1 baño
- garaje

Use expressions such as:

> **Busco un apartamento que tenga . . .**
> **Es importante que . . .**
> **Necesito un apartamento que esté . . .**
> **¿Dónde está?**
> **¿No tiene Ud. algo más . . . ?**

Your partner will begin. You may want to use a piece of paper to take notes.

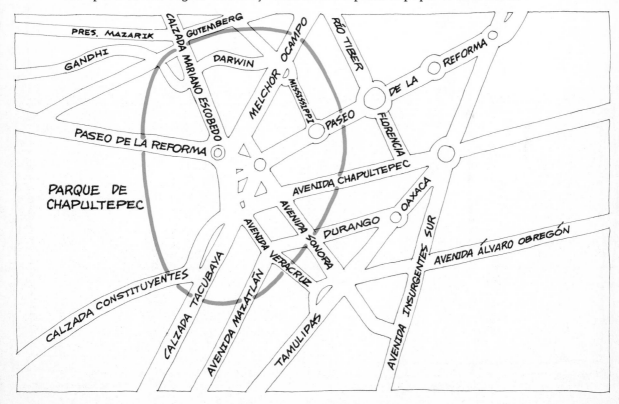

Actividad 19: Las poses

You have to give instructions to your partner so that he/she will make the following pose. This pose is sometimes used to check if someone is drunk. When you are finished, your partner will instruct you on how to do a different pose. Here are some pictures to help you explain your pose. Use expressions such as:

Quiero que levantes la pierna derecha.
Es necesario que cierres la mano . . .
Extiende el brazo derecho.
No levantes el brazo.
¿Qué hago ahora?

You begin by saying: *Es necesario que te levantes y que . . .*

Actividad 20:   Los abogados

You are a lawyer representing Mrs. Romero, who is seeking a divorce. You are discussing the case with her husband's lawyer. Try to reach an amicable agreement as to who gets what. Use expressions such as:

Mi cliente dice que . . .
Ella quiere que él . . .

Your partner will begin.

Here are your case notes:

Cliente: Sara Romero
Caso: Divorcio

La señora dice que su esposo no la ayuda con los niños, gasta mucho dinero y ella no puede dormir por las noches porque su esposo habla mientras duerme. Ella quiere el Mercedes, pero le dará el Audi. Ella pide la casa, "Chuchi" (el dobermán). Hace 10 años que están casados.

Actividad 21:   Los vecinos

You have been very frustrated lately because your neighbors have nine cats and they cause numerous problems. You've tried talking to the owners of the cats, but they just won't listen. You are not a very assertive person. Try to explain some of the problems you have had with the cats to your partner and ask for advice. Your friend has also been having problems where he/she lives and will ask you for advice. Use expressions such as:

> **El otro día los gatos . . .**
> **No sé qué hacer porque ayer . . .**
> **Todas las noches . . .**
> **Te aconsejo que . . .**
> **Quiero que . . .**
> **Es mejor que . . .**

You begin by saying: *Tengo unos problemas terribles con los gatos de mis vecinos.*

Tu problema:

caminar / encima / coche

romper / ropa

hacer ruidos / noche

hacer hoyos / jardín

dejar / animales muertos

Posibles soluciones para tu amigo/a:

tapones para los oídos

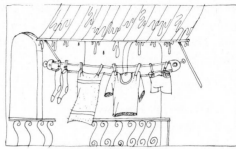

cubrir / ropa / plástico

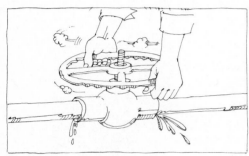

cortarles el agua

cortarles la electricidad

llamar / policía

mudarse

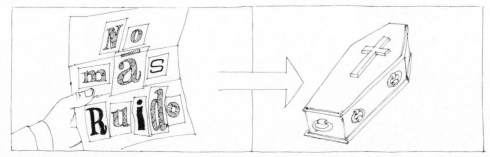

mandarles / carta anónima

You and your brother/sister live in Maracaibo, Venezuela, and would like to host an exchange student for the summer. You have received information on two likely candidates from a student-exchange program. You prefer the young man. Discuss your choice with your brother/sister and decide together which person you want to host.

Useful expressions include:

> **Es preferible que . . .**
> **Es mejor que . . .**
> **Yo prefiero . . . porque . . .**

Your partner will begin.

```
Asociación de Intercambio Estudiantil

Nombre: Bob Lee
Nacionalidad: norteamericano
Ciudad: Manassas, Virginia
Ocupación: estudiante
Edad: 16 años
Pasatiempos: tenis, windsurfing, coleccionar estam-
             pillas, viajar


                                  Manassas, 15 de abril

Querido/a hermano/a de intercambio:

    Me llamo Bob Lee y tengo 16 años. Soy de Manassas,
una pequeña ciudad en los Estados Unidos. Voy a una
escuela secundaria que se llama Osbourn High School.
Hace dos años que estudio español en mi escuela y me
gusta mucho. Escribo español bien pero todavía tengo
problemas cuando quiero hablar. Por eso me gustaría
ir a tu país. Me interesa conocer a personas de otras
culturas y vivir con ellas durante un tiempo.
    Si quieres, puedes escribirme y decirme cómo te
llamas, cuántos años tienes y qué te gusta hacer en
tu tiempo libre.
    Saludos,

    Bob Lee
```

Asociación de Intercambio Estudiantil

Nombre: Janet Chaffee
Nacionalidad: norteamericana
Ciudad: Los Ángeles, California
Ocupación: estudiante
Edad: 17 años
Pasatiempos: montar a caballo, viajar, conocer gente,
            leer novelas de ciencia ficción

                        Los Ángeles 23 de mayo
Querido/a estudiante de intercambio:

    Mi nombre es Janet Chaffee y soy norteamericana.
Tengo 17 años y vivo en Los Ángeles, California. Este
año termino la escuela secundaria y el año que viene
voy a entrar a la universidad. Quiero estudiar so-
ciología pues me gusta mucho aprender sobre la gente
de diferentes partes del mundo. Por eso, quiero ir a
tu país. Me interesa aprender sobre la gente, cómo
vive, qué hace, qué piensa de los Estados Unidos,
etcétera.
    Bueno, si quieres, puedes escribirme y contarme
un poco de ti.
    Saludos,

    Janet Chaffee

Actividad 23:   El reclamo

Your aunt gave you a very expensive leather jacket for **Día de Reyes**, a holiday that is on January 6. It's February and you haven't used your jacket yet. You are two weeks behind in your rent, so YOU NEED MONEY. You decide to go to the store to return the jacket. Fortunately, your aunt gave you the receipt in case you wanted to exchange it.

Use expressions such as:

> **Es necesario que . . .**
> **Es mejor que . . .**
> **Yo necesito que Ud. . . .**

You begin by saying: *Buenos días, quisiera devolver esta chaqueta.*

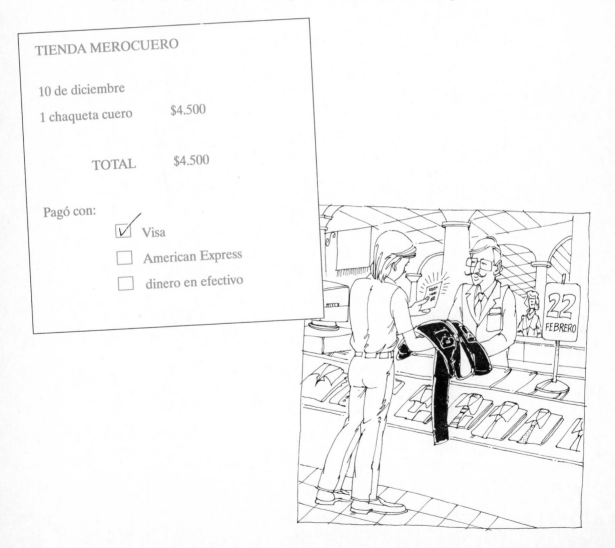

TIENDA MEROCUERO

10 de diciembre

1 chaqueta cuero $4.500

TOTAL $4.500

Pagó con:

- ☑ Visa
- ☐ American Express
- ☐ dinero en efectivo

You are a palm reader. A student comes to you looking for information about some important aspects of his/her future. The following drawing is a guideline for interpretation. Use your imagination and be as specific as possible. Use expressions such as:

Ud. tendrá un futuro . . .
En el amor, Ud. tendrá . . .
Irá . . .
Recibirá . . .
Esta línea aquí . . .

You begin by saying: *Buenas tardes.*

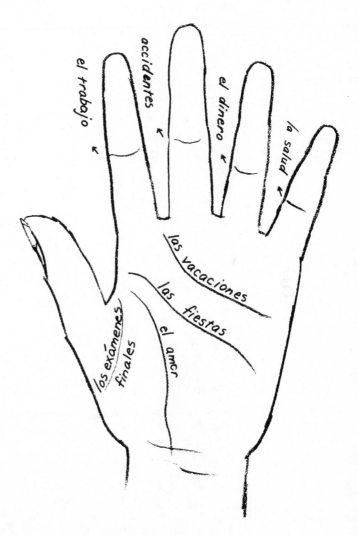

A friend told you about a fortune-teller who is really good. Go to the fortune-teller to find out about your future. He/she uses playing cards in his/her predictions.

Use expressions such as:

> **¿Algo más?**
> **Dígame más.**
> **¿Viajaré mucho?**

Your partner will begin.

These are the cards you may choose from:

Rey de oros

Caballo de copas

Sota de bastos

As de espadas

En parejas 2

Actividad 1: ¿Y tú quién eres?

Fill out the following form with information about yourself.

Nombre: _____ Apellido: _____

Dirección: _____

Ciudad: _____ Teléfono: _____

Casa: _____ Apartamento: _____ Otro: _____

Origen de tu familia: _____

Comida favorita: _____ Actor/actriz favorito/a: _____

Deportes que practicas: _____

Película favorita: _____

Pasatiempo favorito: _____

Asignatura favorita: _____ Asignatura que menos te gusta: _____

Your partner will ask you questions about the above answers. When your partner
finishes, ask him/her questions to complete the following card. Ask questions such
as:

> **¿Cómo te llamas?**
> **¿En qué ciudad vives?**
> **¿Cuál es tu comida favorita?**

Nombre: _____ Apellido: _____

Dirección: _____

Ciudad: _____ Teléfono: _____

Casa: _____ Apartamento: _____ Otro: _____

Origen de tu familia: _____

Comida favorita: _____ Actor/actriz favorito/a: _____

Deportes que practicas: _____

Película favorita: _____

Pasatiempo favorito: _____

Asignatura favorita: _____ Asignatura que menos te gusta: _____

Actividad 2: La cita con el médico

You are Doctor Malahierba's secretary. A patient calls to make an appointment to see the doctor.

Helpful expressions include:

> **El doctor no trabaja por las tardes.**
> **La primera hora libre es a las . . .**
> **La última cita es . . .**
> **Ya tiene otra cita a las . . .**
> **Tiene libre el . . . a las . . .**
> **¿Qué tal el . . . a las . . . ?**

Begin the conversation by saying: *Consultorio, buenos días.*

Here is the doctor's appointment book:

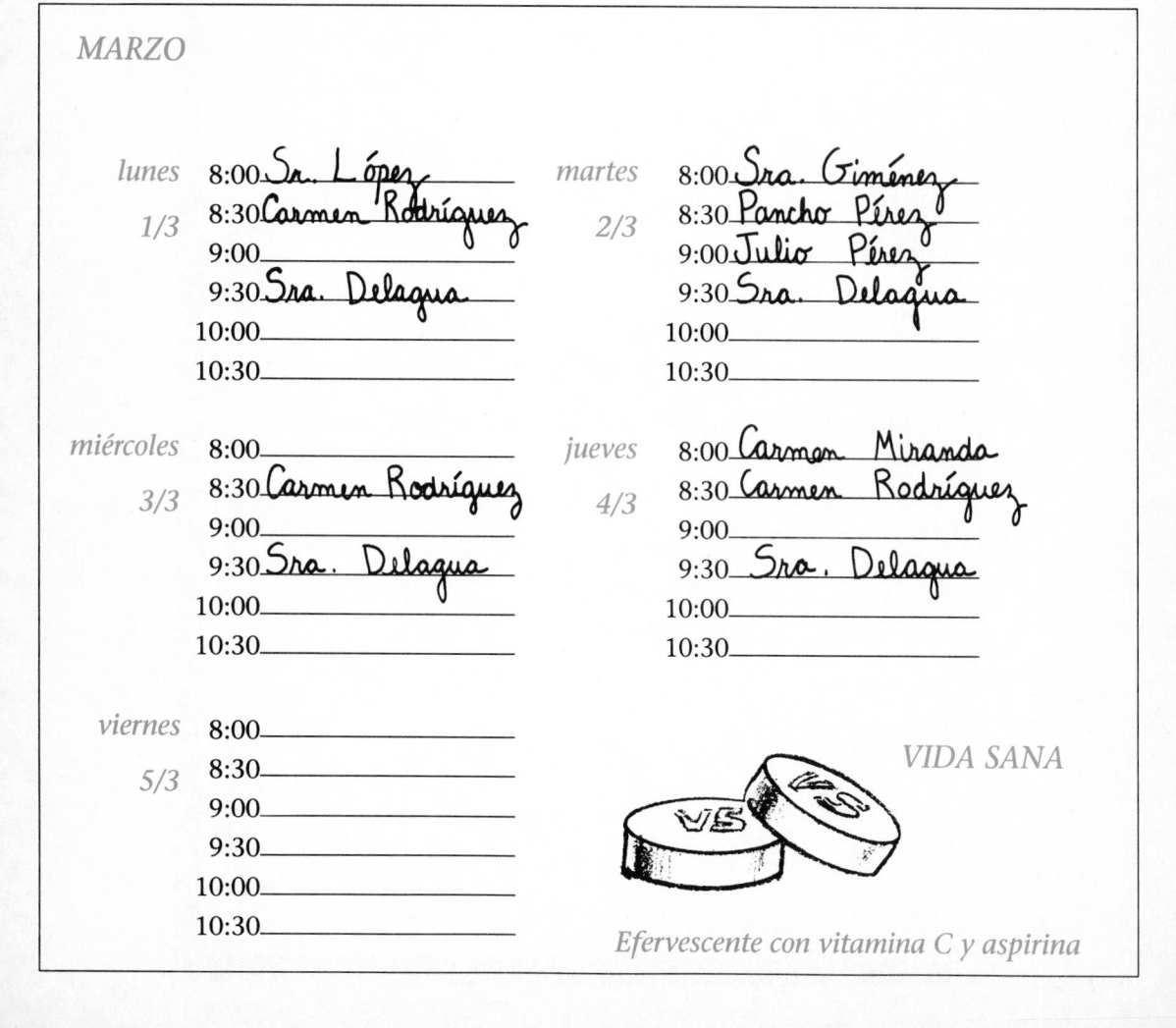

MARZO

lunes
1/3
8:00 Sr. López
8:30 Carmen Rodríguez
9:00
9:30 Sra. Delagua
10:00
10:30

martes
2/3
8:00 Sra. Giménez
8:30 Pancho Pérez
9:00 Julio Pérez
9:30 Sra. Delagua
10:00
10:30

miércoles
3/3
8:00
8:30 Carmen Rodríguez
9:00
9:30 Sra. Delagua
10:00
10:30

jueves
4/3
8:00 Carmen Miranda
8:30 Carmen Rodríguez
9:00
9:30 Sra. Delagua
10:00
10:30

viernes
5/3
8:00
8:30
9:00
9:30
10:00
10:30

VIDA SANA

Efervescente con vitamina C y aspirina

Actividad 3: La cita con el dentista

You call on the telephone to make an appointment with your dentist, Doctora Dientesano. You want to see her as soon as possible, but have a very busy schedule. Use expressions such as:

> **A las 10:00 es imposible porque . . .**
> **No puedo a esa hora porque tengo que . . .**
> **¿Puedo ir el lunes a las . . . ?**
> **Quiero hacer una cita.**

Your partner will begin.

The following is your schedule for the week:

JUNIO

lunes 16/6

5:00-6:30 examen final de cálculo
7:00-8:00 examen oral de inglés

martes 17/6 Después de comer:
- organizar fiesta de cumpleaños. - comprar bebidas y comida para la fiesta
- invitar a mis amigos

miércoles 18/6 ¡Feliz cumpleaños! Hoy es mi cumpleaños. ¡Hoy no hago nada! 4:30 Fiesta en casa

jueves 19/6 3:00-5:30 final de basquetbol por TV

Actividad 4: El coche perfecto

You and your friend have just purchased new cars. Your partner is always bragging about his/her things, but this time you know that your car is better than his/hers. Compare specific features about the two cars. Use expressions such as:

¿Cuántos cilindros . . . ?   El mío tiene más . . .
¿Tiene . . . ?   El tuyo tiene menos . . .
El mío es mejor porque . . .   Me gusta más . . .
El tuyo es peor porque . . .   El mío es tan . . . como el tuyo.

You begin by saying: *¿Sabes que acabo de comprar un coche nuevo?*

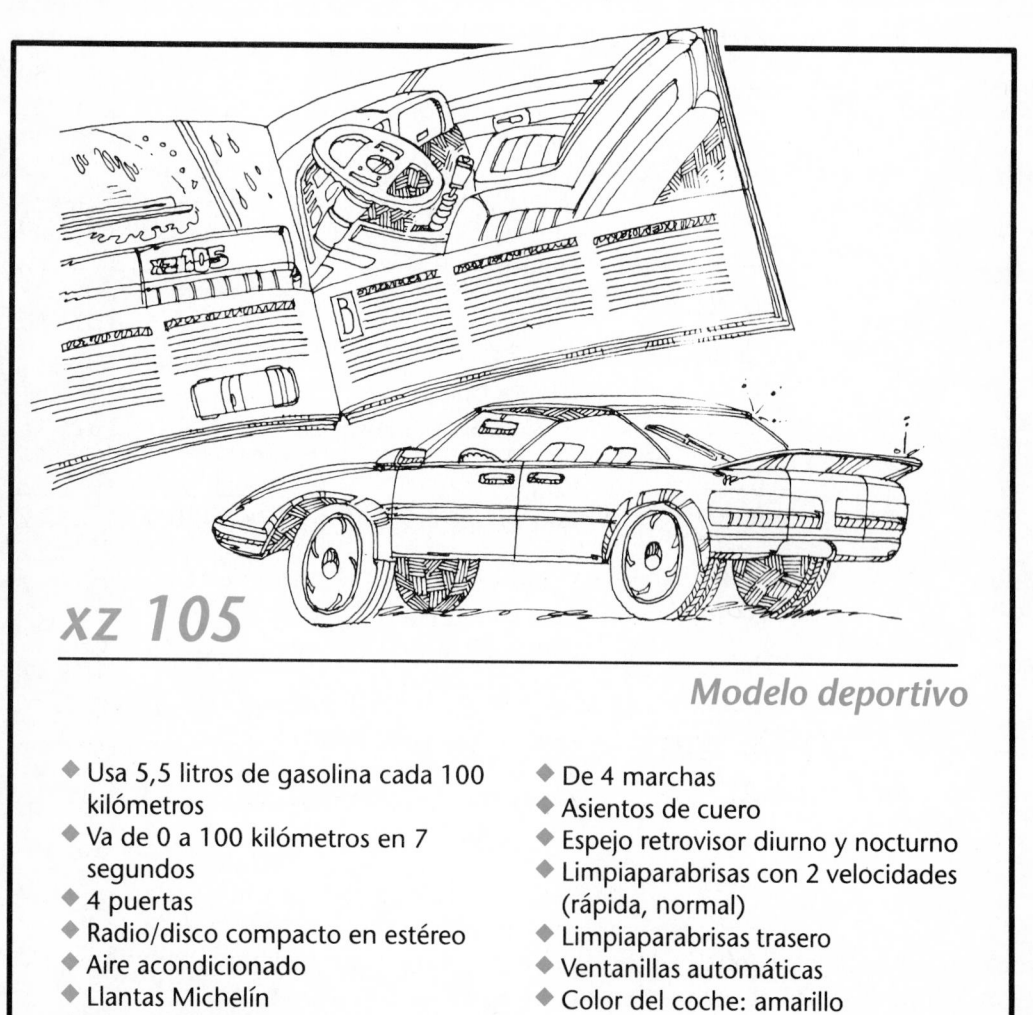

xz 105

Modelo deportivo

- Usa 5,5 litros de gasolina cada 100 kilómetros
- Va de 0 a 100 kilómetros en 7 segundos
- 4 puertas
- Radio/disco compacto en estéreo
- Aire acondicionado
- Llantas Michelín
- Motor de 8 cilindros

- De 4 marchas
- Asientos de cuero
- Espejo retrovisor diurno y nocturno
- Limpiaparabrisas con 2 velocidades (rápida, normal)
- Limpiaparabrisas trasero
- Ventanillas automáticas
- Color del coche: amarillo

Actividad 5:   La tarea

You need to find out some information for your class *Geografiá del hemisferio occidental*. In order to complete your assignment quickly, you split the work with your partner. Find out what your partner has learned from his/her research and complete the chart below. Use phrases such as: **¿Sabes cuántos . . . ?   ¿Me puedes decir cuántos . . . ?**

You begin by asking: *¿Cuántos habitantes tienen los Estados Unidos?*

Estados
Unidos

Brasil

Geografía del hemisferio occidental

Países:	Número de habitantes
Brasil	153.992.000
Estados Unidos	_____
México	88.087.000
Ciudades:	
Nueva York	_____
San Pablo	14.991.000
México	_____
Territorio:	**Kilómetros cuadrados**
Brasil	8.511.965
Canadá	_____
Estados Unidos	9.372.571
sin Alaska y Hawai	7.825.112
Ríos:	**Kilómetros de largo**
Paraná	_____
Amazonas	6.437
Misisipí	_____
Volcanes activos:	**Metros de altura**
Guallatiri, Chile	6.060
Lascar, Chile	_____
Cotopaxi, Ecuador	5.898
Cataratas:	**Metros de altura**
Salto Ángel, Venezuela	_____
Cuquenán, Venezuela	610
King George, Guayana	_____

Now that you have completed the data, quiz each other by trying to formulate and answer some of the questions that might be on the test. For example:

¿Cuál es más grande, . . . o . . . ?   **¿Cuál es el río más . . . ?**
¿Cuál tiene mayor población, . . . o . . . ?   **¿Cuál es más alto/a, . . . ?**

Your partner will begin.

Actividad 6: Objeto olvidado

You work at the front desk of a gym. One of your members comes to claim something that he/she has lost. Ask questions to find out more about what was lost and write out a report. Make sure you get a detailed description of each item. Use expressions such as:

     ¿Cómo era?
     ¿Qué tenía adentro?
     ¿De qué color era . . . ?

Your partner will begin.

GIMNASIO MUSCULÍN
Avda. 6 de Septiembre
Montevideo
Uruguay

Fecha _____

Nombre _____

Dirección _____

Teléfono _____

Objeto(s) perdido(s) _____
_____

Descripción (color, tamaño, cantidad) _____
_____
_____

Dónde _____

Cuándo _____

Comentarios _____
_____

Actividad 7: Objetos perdidos

You have forgotten a suitcase in the cafeteria of a bus station in Chile. You go to the lost-and-found office to claim it. Explain how and where you lost it and describe the contents of the suitcase. Use expressions such as:

La maleta era . . .
Tenía unas medias . . .

You begin by saying: *Olvidé la maleta en la cafetería y quería saber si Ud. la tiene.*

Your partner is thinking of a famous person who is no longer living. You must ask questions to determine which famous person he/she has in mind. The first ten questions must elicit a yes/no response, but after that, you may ask questions to get specific information. When you have figured out who the person is, switch roles.

Useful expressions include:

> **¿Vivió en este siglo?**
> **¿Era abogado / médico / etc.?**
> **¿Tenía pelo rubio / castaño / etc.?**

You may want to make a game of this by awarding a point for each question asked. The person who guesses correctly asking the least number of questions is the winner.

You begin by asking: *¿Era hombre / mujer?*

Some suggestions follow:

Pablo Picasso   Marilyn Monroe

Abraham Lincoln   Miguel de Cervantes

Sammy Davis, Jr.   Martin Luther King, Jr.

Actividad 9:   Mirando fotos

You have just returned from your Christmas vacation with some friends and are discussing your vacation with another friend, who has also just returned from a vacation. You spent five days in Puerto Rico. Tell what the weather was like and what you did each day. Then say whether or not you enjoyed the trip. Base your description on the photos below. Take a few minutes to create details surrounding your trip: who went with you, what you did in each place, how you liked it, etc. Use expressions such as:

Fuimos a . . .   Después . . .
Era muy bonito; había . . .   Al día siguiente . . .
Me gustó porque . . .   Más tarde . . .
Hacía calor; por eso . . .
Mientras nosotros . . . de repente . . .

Your partner will begin.

Día 1   Playa enfrente del hotel

Día 2   La Playa de Luquillo

En parejas 2B

Día 3 Mañana de compras

El Morro-fortaleza en San Juan

Día 4 El Yunque (único bosque pluvial en territorio estadounidense)

Día 5 Huracán

Isla paralizada ¡noche en el lobby!

You used to be very overweight but you went on a strict diet and lost 130 pounds. A feature reporter from the magazine *Gordos Anónimos* is going to interview you about what your life was like before and what it's like now that you have lost weight. Here are some pictures that describe your life and physical appearance both before and after. Use the imperfect to describe what your life used to be like.

Your partner will begin.

ANTES   AHORA

ANTES

AHORA

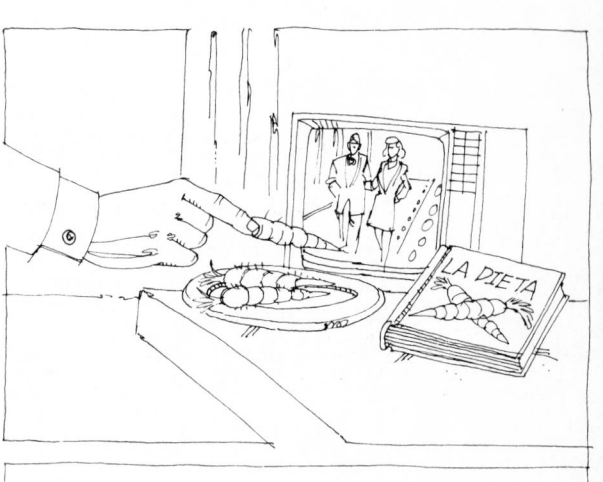

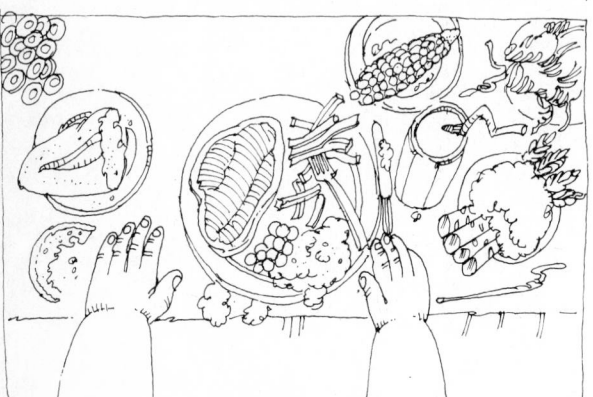

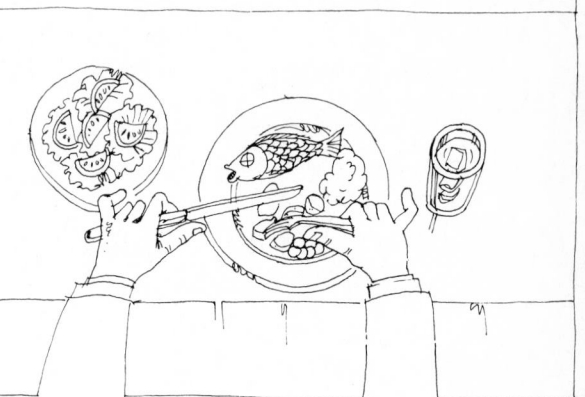

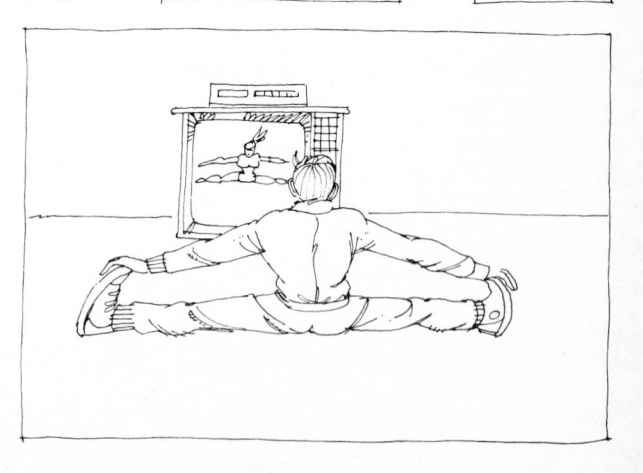

Actividad 11:   La gente curiosa quiere saber

You are a talk show host for the program "Cuéntaselo a millones" and are getting ready to interview a 95–year–old woman. You have been given the following article from a newspaper to help you prepare for the interview. Read it and take a few minutes to jot down some questions.

Divorcio después de 72 años

Elvira Milaños, mujer de 95 años, se divorcia de su esposo después de 72 años de casados. Al preguntarle por qué, ella respondió:

—No voy a decir nada ahora. Sólo voy a hablar en el programa de televisión "Cuéntaselo a millones" este sábado a las 10:00 de la noche. Si Uds. quieren saber por qué me divorcié, tienen que mirar el programa. Lo único que voy a decir ahora es que no podía pasar ni un día más con mi exesposo, Pancracio. ¡Por fin estoy libre!

Todo el mundo quiere saber por qué se divorciaron ahora. Tampoco se sabe qué planes tiene Doña Elvira ahora que está libre. Para obtener las respuestas a éstas y más preguntas, tiene que mirar "Cuéntaselo a millones" este sábado.

Here are a few questions to get you started:

   ¿Cuándo se casaron Uds.?
   ¿Tuvieron hijos?
   ¿Amaba a su esposo cuando Uds. se casaron?

Continue creating questions about why she divorced her husband and what her future plans are.

You begin by saying: **Buenas noches, Doña Elvira. ¿Cómo está Ud.?**

Actividad 12: Contando la historia

Your partner has a series of pictures. You have the four missing pictures your partner needs to complete the story. Together describe your pictures in order to tell the story. When you finish, give the story a title. Use expressions such as:

El hombre fue a correr . . .
(Él) estaba corriendo y de repente . . .
Mientras él corría . . .

Your partner will begin.

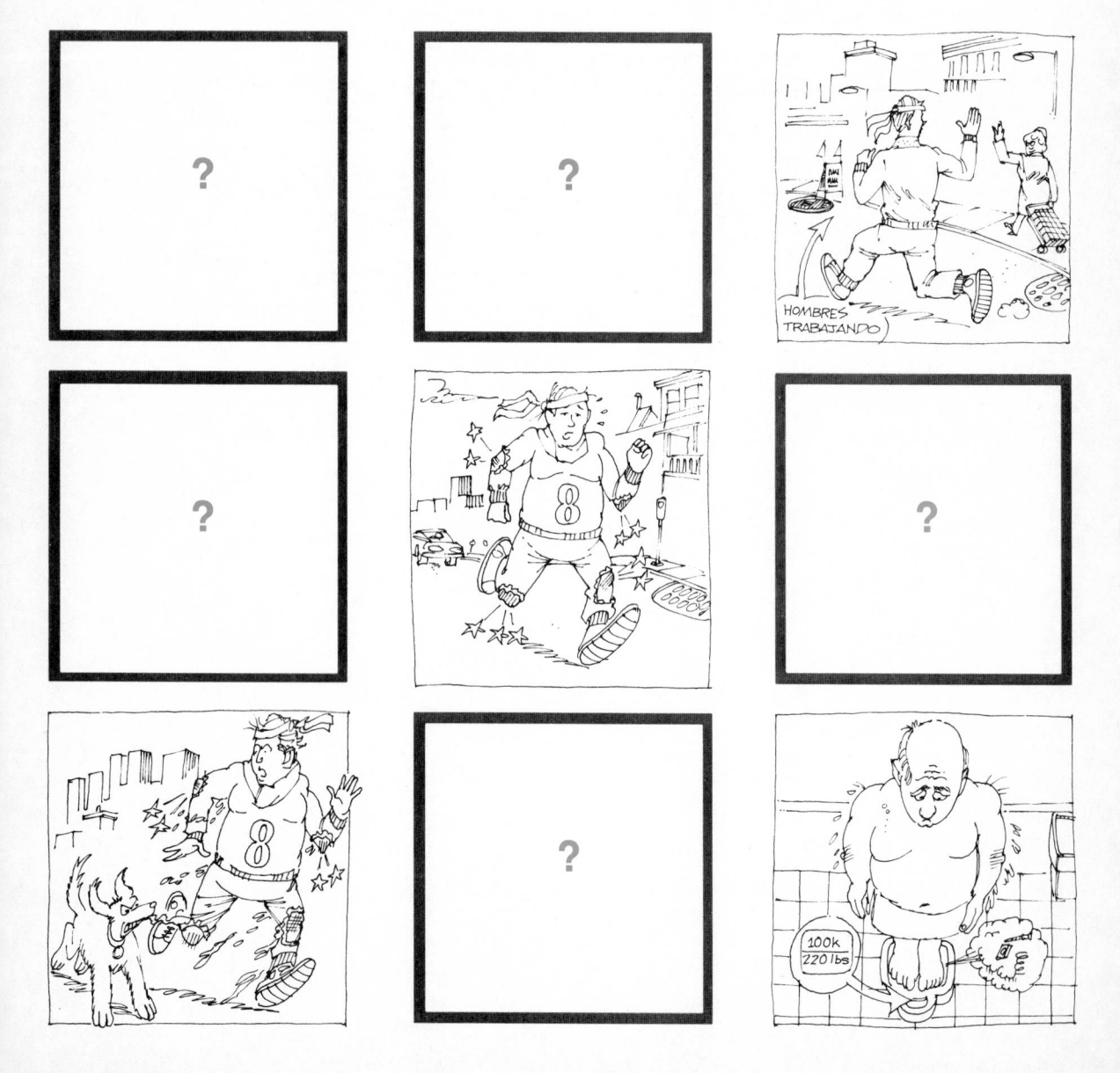

You have a list of expressions below. Your partner has a different list of expressions. You and your partner are going to have a logical conversation about any topic you want. Each of you must try to use all the expressions on your list. You may use them in any order you like. The first to use all the expressions is the winner.

You begin your conversation by saying:

> **Tú:**   **¿Qué hiciste ayer?**
>
> **Tu compañero/a:** . . .
>
> **Tú:**   **Yo también lo pasé bien. ¿Qué hiciste?**
>
> **Tu compañero/a:** . . .
>
> **Tú:**   **???**

Here are the expressions you must use in your conversation:

¿De veras?

Ayer por la mañana . . .

Iba a ir pero . . .

Mientras él . . .

¡No te creo!

Cuando yo tenía 10 años . . .

De repente . . .

El sábado que viene . . .

El mes pasado . . .

Supe la verdad cuando . . .

Actividad 14: Completa el dibujo

Below you have a grid with drawings in some of the boxes. Your partner has the missing drawings. In order to complete the entire grid with the correct drawing in each box, you will need to ask your partner questions. Alternate asking questions to complete your grids. Drawings should be simple. Use stick figures if you like.

To give information, use phrases such as: **Dibuja un/a . . . entre . . .**
                                           Baja dos cuadrados y dobla a la . . .

To ask questions, use phrases such as: ¿Dónde está . . . ?
                                           ¿Está encima de . . . ?
                                           ¿Está a la derecha de . . .?

You begin by saying: *En el segundo cuadrado arriba a la izquierda, dibuja . . .*

Actividad 15: ¿Sabe Ud. dónde está . . . ?

You are at the Hotel Roma in Lima, Peru, and you want to know how to get to the places listed below. You are eating breakfast at the hotel and you ask the person at the next table for directions. You may use expressions such as:

¿Sabe Ud. dónde está . . . ?
¿Puede decirme cómo llegar a . . . ?
Doble a la derecha . . .

Lugares: *Plaza San Martín, Oficina de Turismo, Casa de Cambio, el Correo, el Museo de Cultura Peruana*

Your partner will begin.

¡Ojo! Some streets change names when they cross Unión.

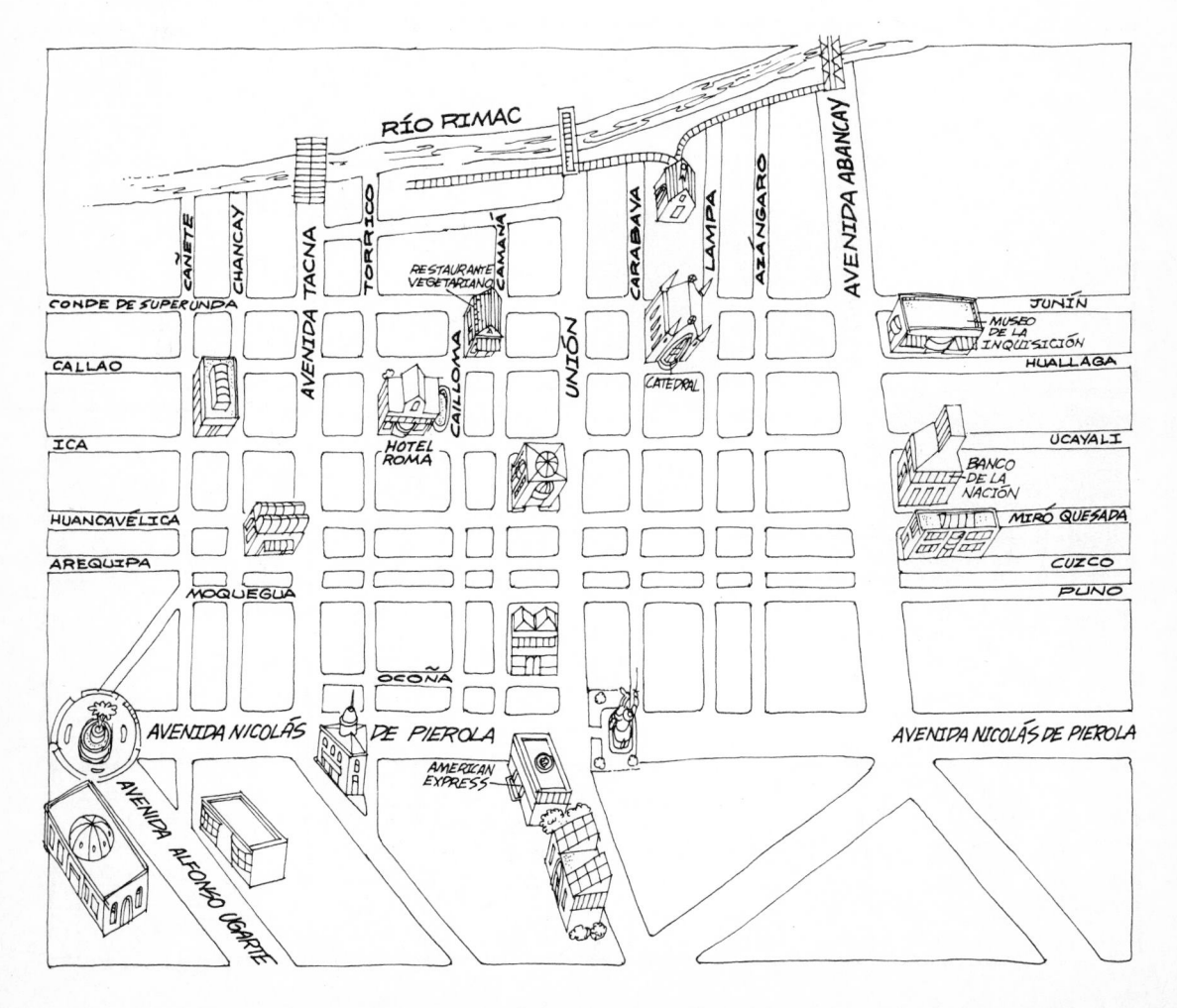

Fill out the following questionnaire about your health and fitness habits. Mark your answers in the box labeled **Tú**.

Your partner will begin.

SALUD GENERAL	dos veces por año		una vez por año		nunca	
	Tú	Comp.	Tú	Comp.	Tú	Comp.
chequeo médico	☐	☐	☐	☐	☐	☐
visita al dentista	☐	☐	☐	☐	☐	☐
tomar vacaciones	☐	☐	☐	☐	☐	☐

MALAS COSTUMBRES	nunca		poco		mucho	
	Tú	Comp.	Tú	Comp.	Tú	Comp.
fumar	☐	☐	☐	☐	☐	☐
beber café	☐	☐	☐	☐	☐	☐
usar sal	☐	☐	☐	☐	☐	☐
tomar bebidas alcohólicas	☐	☐	☐	☐	☐	☐

	8-10 horas cada noche		6-8 horas cada noche		menos de 6 horas cada noche	
	Tú	Comp.	Tú	Comp.	Tú	Comp.
dormir	☐	☐	☐	☐	☐	☐

EJERCICIO FÍSICO	todos los días		tres veces por semana		una vez por semana	
	Tú	Comp.	Tú	Comp.	Tú	Comp.
nadar	☐	☐	☐	☐	☐	☐
correr	☐	☐	☐	☐	☐	☐

When you have finished, answer your partner's questions and then ask about his/her habits. Mark his/her responses in the box labeled **Comp**.

Once you are finished, total the results and compare your score with your partner's. Follow the instructions below to arrive at your totals and to interpret your answers.

Puntuación de las respuestas:

Por cada marca en la primera columna recibes 3 puntos.

Por cada marca en la segunda columna recibes 2 puntos.

Por cada marca en la tercera columna no recibes ningún punto.

Escribe el total de los puntos de tu parte de la prueba: _____

Escribe el total de los puntos de tu compañero/a: _____

30–25	Eres muy saludable. Puedes saltar edificios con un solo salto.
24–19	Llevas una vida sana, pero hay cositas que debes cambiar.
18–13	Debes hacer citas urgentemente con un dentista y un médico. Después debes cambiar tu dieta y matricularte en una clase de ejercicios aeróbicos.
12–7	Tienes problemas. Si no cambias tus malas costumbres vas a tener que visitar al médico pero no en su consultorio sino en la sala de emergencias.
0–6	¿Dijiste la verdad al contestar las preguntas? Sugiero que tomes unas vacaciones largas y que reexamines tu ritmo de vida. Tienes que cambiar tus malas costumbres o pagar el precio con tu salud.

Decide which of you leads a healthier life and give your partner advice to help improve his/her lifestyle. Use expressions such as:

Es mejor que tú . . .
Te aconsejo que . . .
Es necesario que . . .

Actividad 17:   Decorando

You are an interior designer and have been working on a design for your client's living room. Call your assistant and describe what you have planned so that he/she can put the furniture in the correct places. Use expressions such as: **Quiero que pongas la mesa . . .   A la derecha quiero que . . .   Pon la mesa enfrente de . . .**

Your partner will begin.

Actividad 18:   Buscando apartamento

You work for a real-estate agency in Mexico City. A customer calls you looking for a one-bedroom apartment. Find out what he/she is looking for and what part of the city would be best. Here is a list of the apartments you have available now. Their locations are indicated on the map. Use expressions such as:

¿Dónde le gustaría . . . ?
Tengo uno muy bonito que está en la calle . . . entre las calles . . .
¿Le molesta no tener . . . ?
No tengo ninguno que tenga / esté . . .
¿A qué hora puede Ud. . . . ?

You begin by answering the phone: *Inmobiliaria Alquilatodo, buenos días.*

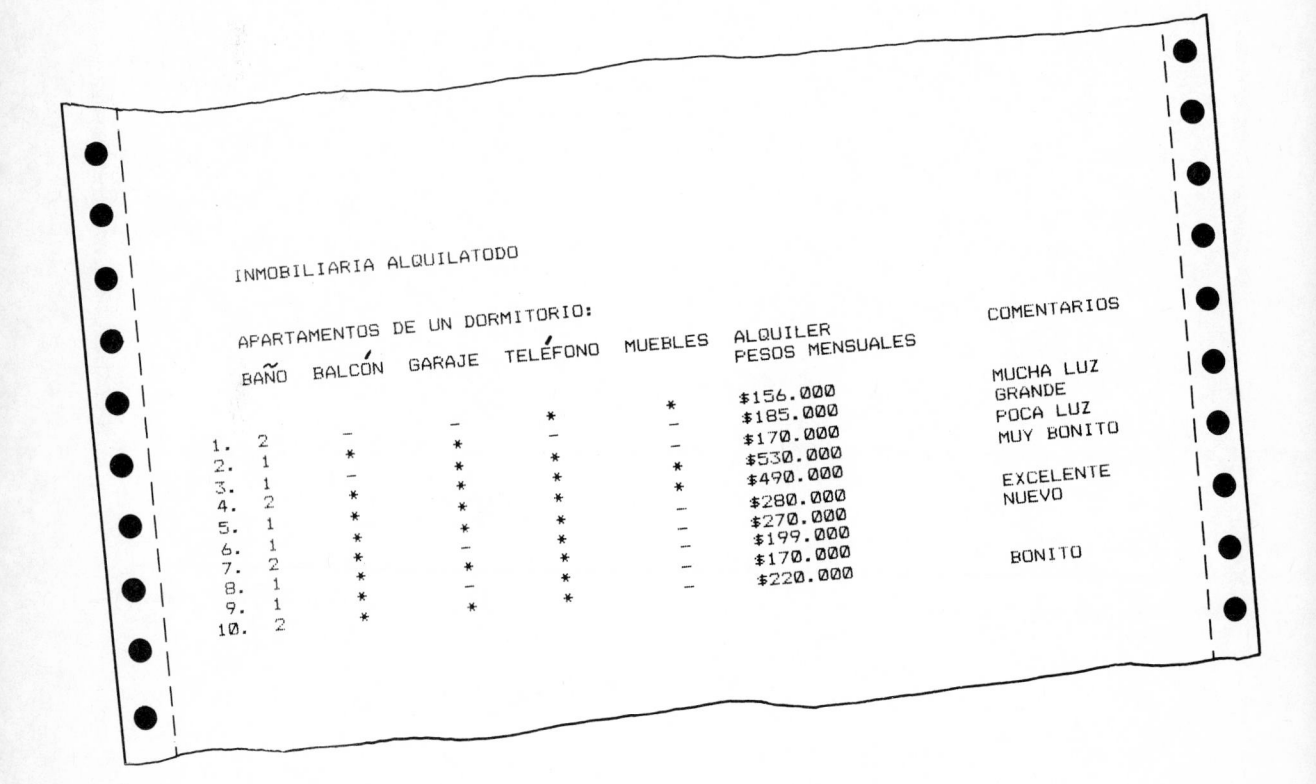

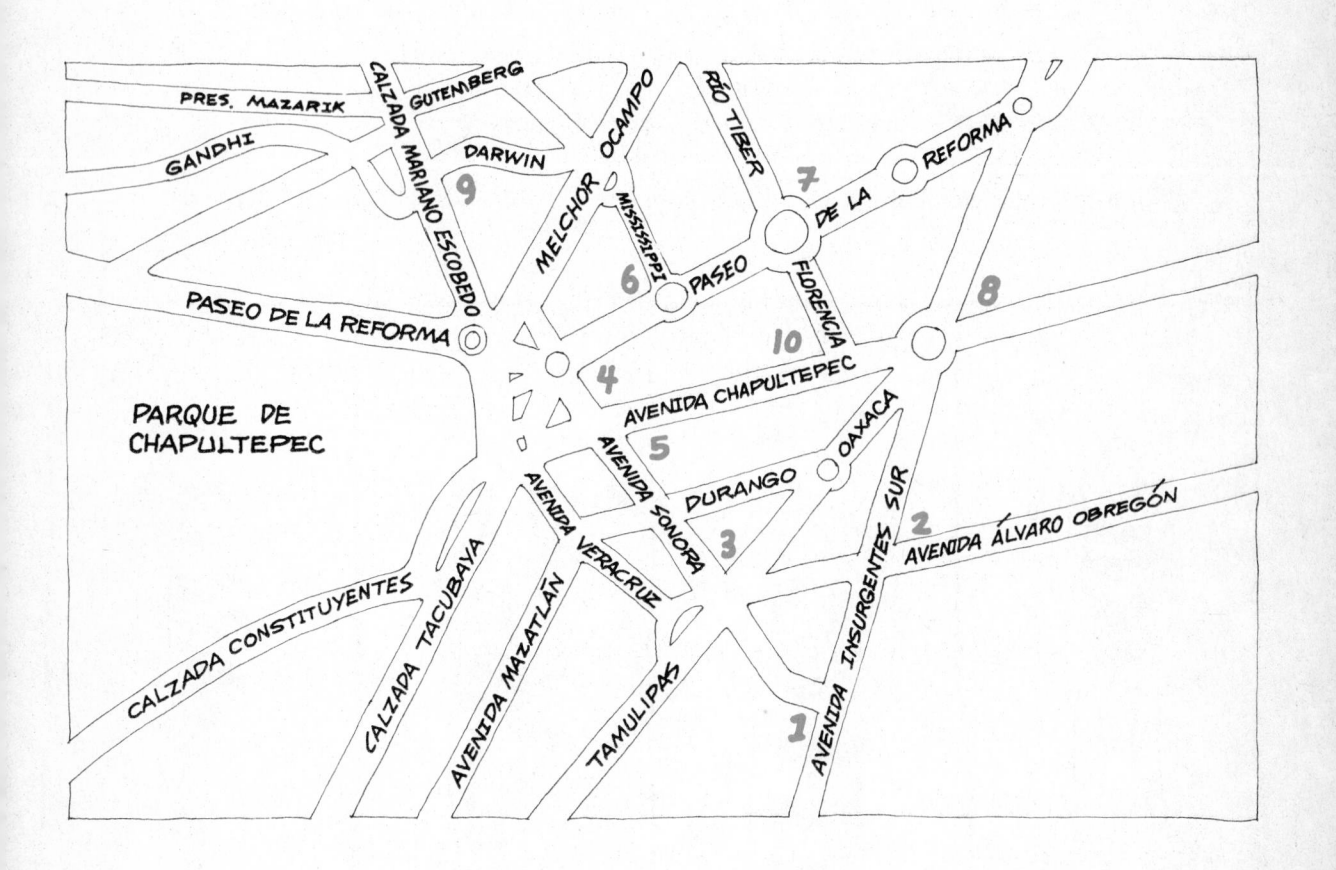

PARQUE DE
CHAPULTEPEC

PRES. MAZARIK

GANDHI

CALZADA MARIANO ESCOBEDO

CALZADA GUTEMBERG

DARWIN

9

MELCHOR OCAMPO

MISSISSIPPI

6

RÍO TIBER

7

PASEO

DE LA REFORMA

FLORENCIA

8

PASEO DE LA REFORMA

4

AVENIDA CHAPULTEPEC

5

OAXACA

DURANGO

3

AVENIDA SONORA

10

AVENIDA VERACRUZ

AVENIDA MAZATLÁN

CALZADA TACUBAYA

CALZADA CONSTITUYENTES

TAMULIPAS

AVENIDA INSURGENTES SUR

2

AVENIDA ÁLVARO OBREGÓN

1

Your partner is going to give you instructions. Do exactly what he/she tells you to do. When you are finished, give instructions to your partner to make the following pose, which will test his/her balance. Here are some pictures to help you explain the pose. Use expressions such as:

>**Quiero que levantes los brazos.**
>**Toma la muñeca . . .**
>**Levanta la pierna derecha.**
>**Es necesario que cruces** (*cross*) **la pierna derecha sobre . . .**
>**¿Qué hago ahora?**

Your partner will begin.

You are a lawyer representing Mr. Romero, who is seeking a divorce. You are discussing the case with his wife's lawyer. Try to reach an amicable agreement as to who gets what. Use expressions such as:

Mi cliente dice que . . .
Él quiere que ella . . .

You begin by saying: **Buenos días, soy . . .**

Here are your case notes:

Cliente: Alfredo Romero
Caso: Divorcio
Dice que su esposa trabaja todo el día, ronca toda la noche y no puede dormir.
Hace 10 años que están casados.
Cliente quiere: el apartamento de tiempo compartido en Suiza, "Chuchi" (el dobermán), la colección de discos. Él quiere el Mercedes, pero le dará el Audi.

You are having some problems with your upstairs neighbors. Your friend is also having problems and he/she is coming to your house for some advice. Listen to him/her and give advice. You may use the drawings below to help you. Then explain your problem to see if your friend can help. Use expressions such as:

Todas las noches . . .
No sé qué hacer porque anoche . . .
Te aconsejo que . . .
Quiero que . . .
Es mejor que. . .

Your partner will begin.

Posibles soluciones para tu amigo/a:

mudarse   pistola de agua   darles veneno   ponerlos / jaula

llamar / policía   ponerles un pleito a los vecinos   perro

echar agua a las plantas
/mojar / ropa

fiestas / fines de semana

loro / hablar

peleas / todas las noches

cantar / ducha

Actividad 22: El/La estudiante de intercambio

You and your brother/sister live in Maracaibo, Venezuela, and would like to host an exchange student for the summer. You have received information on two likely candidates from a student-exchange program. You prefer the young woman. Discuss your choice with your brother/sister and decide together which person you want to host.

Useful expressions include:
Es preferible que . . .
Es mejor que . . .
Yo prefiero . . . porque . . .

You will begin.

Asociación de Intercambio Estudiantil

Nombre: Bob Lee
Nacionalidad: norteamericano
Ciudad: Manassas, Virginia
Ocupación: estudiante
Edad: 16 años
Pasatiempos: tenis, windsurfing, coleccionar estam-
             pillas, viajar

Manassas, 15 de abril

Querido/a hermano/a de intercambio:

Me llamo Bob Lee y tengo 16 años. Soy de Manassas, una pequeña ciudad en los Estados Unidos. Voy a una escuela secundaria que se llama Osbourn High School. Hace dos años que estudio español en mi escuela y me gusta mucho. Escribo español bien pero todavía tengo problemas cuando quiero hablar. Por eso me gustaría ir a tu país. Me interesa conocer a personas de otras culturas y vivir con ellas durante un tiempo.
Si quieres, puedes escribirme y decirme cómo te llamas, cuántos años tienes y qué te gusta hacer en tu tiempo libre.
Saludos,

Bob Lee

Asociación de Intercambio Estudiantil

Nombre: Janet Chaffee
Nacionalidad: norteamericana
Ciudad: Los Ángeles, California
Ocupación: estudiante
Edad: 17 años
Pasatiempos: montar a caballo, viajar, conocer gente,
             leer novelas de ciencia ficción

                                    Los Ángeles 23 de mayo

Querido/a estudiante de intercambio:

    Mi nombre es Janet Chaffee y soy norteamericana.
Tengo 17 años y vivo en Los Ángeles, California. Este
año termino la escuela secundaria y el año que viene
voy a entrar a la universidad. Quiero estudiar so-
ciología pues me gusta mucho aprender sobre la gente
de diferentes partes del mundo. Por eso, quiero ir a
tu país. Me interesa aprender sobre la gente, cómo
vive, qué hace, qué piensa de los Estados Unidos,
etcétera.
    Bueno, si quieres, puedes escribirme y contarme
un poco de ti.
    Saludos,

        Janet Chaffee

Actividad 23: El reclamo

Today is February 22 and you have been working for one week at Merocuero, a store that specializes in leather clothing. Your boss is very strict and is always breathing down your neck. Fortunately, he called in sick today. He warned you over the phone to follow store policies to the letter and told you to call him if you had any questions. You want to avoid calling him about anything. Use expressions such as:

Es imposible que . . .
No es posible que . . .

Your partner will begin.

Here is a list of the store policies:

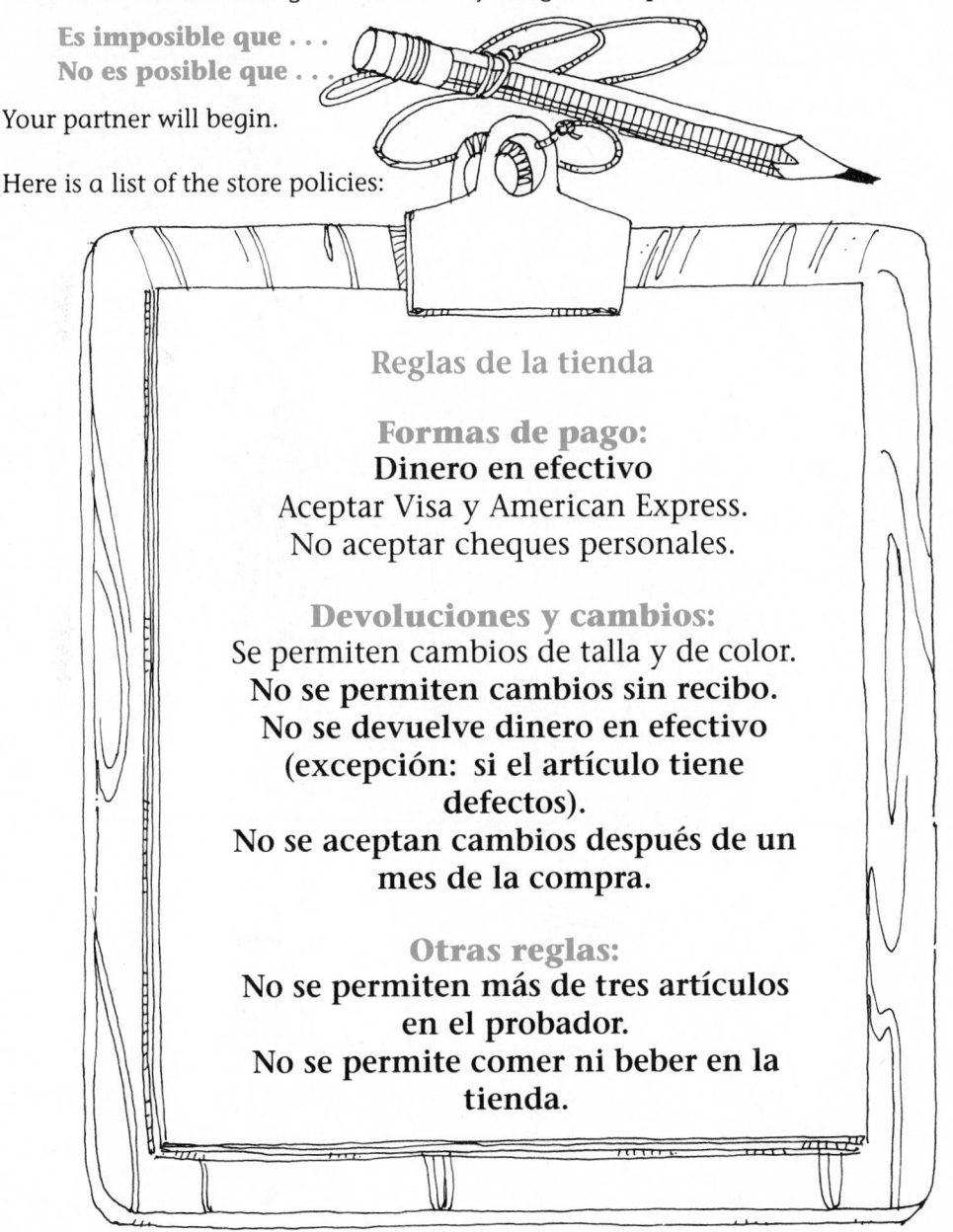

Reglas de la tienda

Formas de pago:
Dinero en efectivo
Aceptar Visa y American Express.
No aceptar cheques personales.

Devoluciones y cambios:
Se permiten cambios de talla y de color.
No se permiten cambios sin recibo.
No se devuelve dinero en efectivo
(excepción: si el artículo tiene
defectos).
No se aceptan cambios después de un
mes de la compra.

Otras reglas:
No se permiten más de tres artículos
en el probador.
No se permite comer ni beber en la
tienda.

Actividad 24: Tu futuro en la palma de la mano

You believe in the supernatural and want to know what lies ahead in your future so you go to see a palm reader. Use expressions such as:

> **¿Qué ocurrirá en mi vida?**
> **¿Tendré muchos hijos?**

Your partner will begin.

Actividad 25: **Tu futuro en las cartas**

You are a fortune-teller who predicts the future using playing cards. To predict the future you follow this procedure: you say a category, such as **dinero**, and the client selects a card; you then base your prediction on the card selected for the category. Use your imagination to create details. Useful expressions include:

> **Ud. tendrá . . .**
> **Ud. viajará a . . .**
> **Será . . .**

You begin by saying: *Las cartas nos dirán su futuro.*

Sota de bastos	Caballo de copas	Rey de oros	As de espadas
			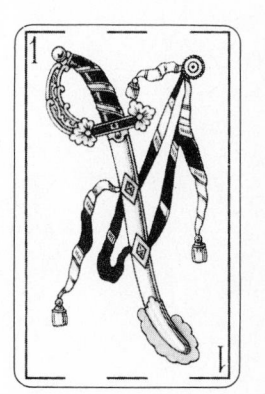

	Sota de bastos	Caballo de copas	Rey de oros	As de espadas
Salud:	accidente	buena	hospital	operación
Dinero:	lotería	robo	poco	mucho
Trabajo:	sensacional	perder	banco	internacional
Amor:	boda	muchos amores	2	divorcio
Hijos:	0	9	2	3
Viajes:	África	Las Vegas	0	todo el mundo

NOTAS NOTAS NOTAS NOTAS NOTAS NOTAS NOTAS NOTAS NOTAS NOTAS

NOTAS NOTAS NOTAS NOTAS NOTAS NOTAS NOTAS NOTAS NOTAS NOTAS

NOTAS NOTAS NOTAS NOTAS NOTAS NOTAS NOTAS NOTAS NOTAS

NOTAS NOTAS NOTAS NOTAS NOTAS NOTAS NOTAS NOTAS NOTAS NOTAS

NOTAS NOTAS NOTAS NOTAS NOTAS NOTAS NOTAS NOTAS NOTAS

NOTAS NOTAS NOTAS NOTAS NOTAS NOTAS NOTAS NOTAS NOTAS NOTAS